Plants

Kay Davies
and
Wendy Oldfield

Wayland

Starting Science

Books in the series

Animals
Day and Night
Electricity and Magnetism
Floating and Sinking
Food
Hot and Cold
Information Technology
Light
Local Ecology
Materials

Plants
Pushing and Pulling
Rocks and Soil
The Senses
Skeletons and Movement
Sound and Music
Time and Change
Waste
Water
Weather

About this book

Plants involves children in a variety of investigations to find out about plants and the conditions necessary for their growth. Simple plant and flower parts are named and their functions looked at. Children learn about seeds and other ways that plants reproduce themselves, including the spores produced by non-flowering plants.

This book provides an introduction to methods in scientific enquiry and recording. The activities and investigations are designed to be straightforward but fun, and flexible according to the abilities of the children. The main picture and its commentary may be taken as an introduction to the topic or as a focal point for further discussion. Each chapter can form a basis for extended topic work.

Teachers will find that in using this book, they are reinforcing the other core subjects of language and mathematics. Through its topic approach **Plants** covers aspects of the original National Science Curriculum for key stage 1 (levels 1 to 3), for the following Attainment Targets: Exploration of science (AT 1), The variety of life (AT 2) and Processes of life (AT 3) as well as for the amended Curriculum: Scientific investigation (AT 1) and Life and living processes (AT 2).

First published in 1992 by
Wayland (Publishers) Ltd
61 Western Road, Hove
East Sussex BN3 1JD, England

© Copyright 1992 Wayland (Publishers) Ltd

Typeset by Kalligraphic Design Ltd, Surrey
Printed in Italy by
  Rotolito Lombarda S.p.A., Milan
Bound in Belgium by Casterman S.A.

British Library Cataloguing in Publication Data
Davies, Kay 1946
  1. Plants (Starting science)
  I. Title II. Oldfield, Wendy
  III. Archer, Rebecca IV. Series
  581

ISBN 0 7502 0287 4

Editor: Cally Chambers

CONTENTS

Plant parts	4
Food factories	7
Light fantastic	9
Well watered	10
New growth	12
A place to grow	15
Hothouse	17
Flower festival	18
Carried away	21
Hitching a ride	22
Spores galore!	24
Safe in store	27
Take a cutting	28
Glossary	30
Finding out more	31
Index	32

All the words that first appear in **bold** in the text are explained in the glossary.

PLANT PARTS

Many plants have flowers. Their **petals** are often brightly coloured.

The **stem** holds the plant upright. It carries water and food to the branches and leaves.

Most plants have **roots**. They reach into the soil to take in water and goodness. They fix the plant in the ground.

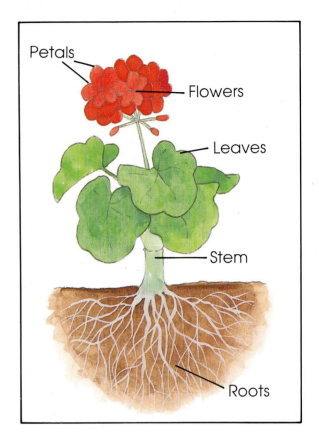

Dig up a dandelion with its roots.

Lay it on white paper and draw around the whole plant.

Colour in your drawing.

Make labels for each part. Stick them on your picture.

The wild wind has blown down the trees. We can see their roots as well as their trunks, branches and leaves.

The water-lilies have huge green leaves. They float on the water catching lots of light from the sun.

FOOD FACTORIES

Leaves are different shapes and sizes. How many different ones can you count here? Leaves are very important to plants. A special green substance inside them uses sunlight to make plants grow.

Some plants rest in winter. They don't need to make food then. So they lose their leaves in the autumn.

Collect some leaves.

It's fun to draw around the different shapes and colour them in.

Find out the names of the plants your leaves came from. Make a leaf book.

Use some leaves to make a picture for your wall.

There are many trees in the forest. They grow tall and thin as they grow up towards the light.

LIGHT FANTASTIC

All plants need sunlight to grow. They grow towards it.

Only those that have enough light can make food to grow tall and strong.

In spring, fill three flowerpots with soil. Plant a few marigold seeds in each. Put one in a dark cupboard, one on a windowsill and leave one in a shady place.

Water your seeds when the soil dries out. Look at them often. Do all the seeds grow?

Do your plants look the same? What happens to the plants on the windowsill if you turn the pot around?

What do you notice about the seeds left in the dark? What happens to the seeds left in the shade?

WELL WATERED

All plants need water to live.

We have to water our house plants to keep them alive. The plants in our gardens and on our farms need to be watered in hot dry summers.

Cut some flowers.

Leave some in an empty vase.
Leave some in a vase with water.

Which flowers keep their shape and colour the longest?

Dig up two plants with roots. Chop the roots off one of them.

Leave both plants in jars of water.
Which one **wilts** first?

Roots take water up into the plant and help it to live longer.

The spiky cacti are used to growing in the dry desert. But the flowers have to wait for rain to make them grow.

NEW GROWTH

Most plants make new plants that look like themselves. Some send out long shoots and some make seeds.

Soak some beans in water overnight.
Fill a glass jar with **damp** peat.

Plant your beans about 3 cm deep.
Put some on their sides and some straight up.
Put them round the sides of the jar so that you can see them.

Keep the peat damp.
Do all of your beans grow roots?
Do the roots always grow the same way?
Do they grow up or down?

Your beans will grow stems as well as roots.

Which grow first, the roots or the stems?

Look at all the beans. They are hard, dry seeds that must soak up water before they can grow into new plants.

The tractor's plough turns over the soil and breaks it up. New plants will have a good place to grow.

A PLACE TO GROW

All seeds need a place to **germinate** and soil to grow in.

Some plants can grow in the dry desert sands. Some can grow in wet **marshlands**.

Some grow on the leafy jungle floor and some on the bare mountain soil.

Seeds grow into plants in many different places.

Find seven shallow trays. Fill each tray with something different. Try sand, soil, sawdust, pebbles, flour, shredded paper and polystyrene. Water each tray and spread mustard and cress seeds in them.

Keep the trays damp. Leave them in the light. Do all your seeds germinate and grow well?

The warmth of the sun is trapped inside the hothouse. The young plants have everything they need for growth.

HOTHOUSE

Plants need light, water and a place to grow. The **temperature** of the air and soil is important too.

Plant some seeds in two flowerpots.

Ask an adult to cut a large see-through, plastic bottle in half.

Use the top half to cover one flowerpot. It is like a small **hothouse**.

Leave both pots outside where there is plenty of light.

Water your seeds every day.

Which seeds germinate first?

Do the seeds in both pots grow just as well?

FLOWER FESTIVAL

The lovely colours and **scents** from flowers attract lots of insects.

Insects feed on **nectar** inside the flower. Yellow **pollen** dust from flowers sticks to their bodies and is carried from flower to flower.

The pollen will help the flowers to make fruits and seeds.

Collect different flowers. Can you find the pollen?

Count the petals on each flower. Do they all have the same number?

Pull some petals off the flowers. Leave them to dry in a warm place.

Crush the petals when they are dry. Can you smell their lovely scent?

The float has been decorated with colourful flowers. Can you see what they have been made into?

The poppy flowers have died. The dry heads shake in the wind and scatter their tiny seeds far and wide.

CARRIED AWAY

Seeds grow best away from each other. They need space to grow.

Some plants have seed pods which explode. The seeds are thrown into the air.
Some seeds are feathery and float away in the wind.
Some have wings to carry them away.

Throw maple or sycamore seeds into the air. Watch them spin away. You can make a spinner like this:

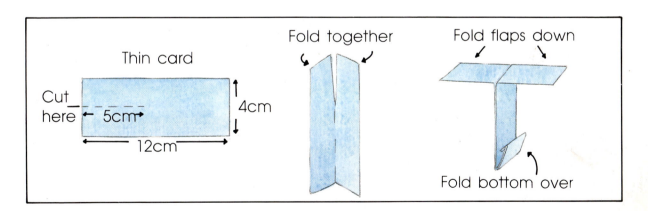

Test your spinner by twisting it into the air.
Now try making the cut different lengths. Does it spin better with a paperclip weight at the bottom?

HITCHING A RIDE

Some seeds have spines or hooks.
They catch on animals' fur or people's clothes and are carried away.

They may fall off into the soil and grow into new plants.

Birds may eat some seeds and spread them in their droppings.

We might spread seeds from the soil with our shoes.

After a walk in the country or park, ask your friends to scrape the soil from their shoes.

Mix each sample in a pot with some compost and water.
Cover them with a clear plastic sheet.
Whose shoes collected the most seeds?

Birds like to eat the bright berries. As they fly around, their droppings spread the berries' seeds.

SPORES GALORE!

Seaweeds, lichens, mosses and ferns do not have flowers. They make **spores**.

Non-flowering plants like these often grow in wet or damp places.

Most spores are far too tiny to see with our eyes.

But the spores of garden ferns are big enough for us to see.

Cut some ferns and put them in a vase of water.

Stand the vase on a large piece of white paper. Look at the paper every day.
Can you see the tiny brown spores as they fall from the plant?
Can you find which part of the plant they have come from?

The seaweeds have no flowers. Instead of seeds they have spores which float away and make new plants.

The shop is full of all sorts of **bulbs**. People like to buy them and grow them into colourful flowers.

SAFE IN STORE

Some plants can grow from bulbs as well as seeds.

An onion flower makes many seeds. Each seed can grow into a new plant.

Every year the old onion plant grows up from a bulb. Food made by the leaves makes the base of the plant swell into a fat bulb.

In winter the leaves die but the bulb rests in the soil. The bulb will grow into a new plant in spring.

Look at an onion bulb. Has it got roots?

Ask an adult to cut it in half. Is it juicy inside? Can you see the layers of leaves?

These flowers grow from bulbs. Can you name them?

1. Daffodil
2. Tulip
3. Hyacinth
4. Snowdrop

TAKE A CUTTING

Plants can grow from seeds and from bulbs.
We can make new plants grow in other ways too.

Find a busy Lizzy plant with lots of stems.

With some friends, cut off a few stems with leaves.

Each put your stem in a jar of water. Make sure that the leaves are above the water level.

Leave your busy Lizzy **cuttings** and look at them often.

Whose cutting grows roots first?

Plant your rooted cuttings in soil. Press the soil down firmly with your hands. You will each have your own new plant.
It will be exactly like the plant it was cut from.

Many of the young plants in the nursery have been grown from cuttings. People buy them for their gardens.

GLOSSARY

Bulb A rounded part of some plants that grows underground.
Cuttings Plant stems that can be grown into new plants.
Damp Slightly wet.
Germinate To start growing from a seed.
Hothouse A place where plants can grow at a warm and even temperature. Also called a greenhouse.
Marshlands Lands that are always wet.
Nectar A sweet juice, made inside a flower, that insects like to drink.
Non-flowering plants Plants that do not have flowers. They make new plants from spores.
Nursery A place where people grow new plants for gardens.
Petals The outside, coloured parts of a flower.
Plough A machine for turning over the soil before planting.
Pollen The yellow dust in a flower that starts fruits and seeds growing.
Roots The parts of a plant which take up water and goodness from the soil.
Scent A nice smell.
Spores The seeds of non-flowering plants.
Stem The part of a plant that carries goodness to the leaves and flowers.
Temperature How hot or cold something is.
Wilt To go floppy. A plant wilts when it doesn't have enough water.

FINDING OUT MORE

Books to read:

My Apple by Kay Davies and Wendy Oldfield (A & C Black, 1990)
Plants by Alain Gree (Franklin Watts, 1990)
Local Ecology by Kay Davies and Wendy Oldfield (Wayland, 1992)

Series that include useful books:

Experiment With Things That Grow (Collins)
Life Cycles (Wayland)
Nature Study (Wayland)
The Seasons (Wayland)
The Stopwatch Books (A & C Black)
Use Your Eyes (Wayland)

PICTURE ACKNOWLEDGEMENTS

Chris Fairclough 24; Hutchison 26; J. Allan Cash Ltd 29; Oxford Scientific Films 23; Tony Stone Worldwide 6, 8, 13, 14, 16, 20; Topham 5, 19; Wayland Picture Library (Zul Mukhida) *cover*, 4, 7, 10 top and bottom, 12, 15, 17, 18, 22, 27, 28; ZEFA 11, 25.

Artwork illustrations by Rebecca Archer.
The publishers would also like to thank the parents and children for their kind co-operation in making this book.

INDEX

Page numbers in **bold** indicate subjects shown in pictures, but not mentioned in the text on those pages.

Beans 12, 13
Berries **22**, 23
Branches 4, 5
Bulbs 26, 27, 28

Cuttings 28, 29, 30

Desert 11, 15

Flowers 4, 10, 11, 18, 19, 20, 24, 25, 26, 27
Food 4, 9, 27
Fruits 18

Gardens 10, 24, 29
Germinate 15, 17, 30
Growth 7, 8, 9, 11, 12, 13, 14, 16, 17, 21, 22

Hothouse 16, 17, 30

Jungle 15

Leaves 4, 5, 6, 7, 15, 27, 28
Lichens 24

Marshland 15, 30

Nectar 18, 30
Nursery 29, 30

Petals 4, 18, 30

Plants
  busy Lizzy 28
  cacti 11, **15**
  daffodil 27
  dandelions 4, **21**
  ferns 24
  hyacinth 27
  marigolds 9
  mosses 24
  poppies 20
  snowdrop 27
  tulip 27
  water-lilies 6

Roots 4, 5, 10, 12, 27, 28, 30

Scent 18, 30
Seaweed 24, 25
Seeds 9, 12, 13, 15, 17, 18, 20, 21, 23, 27, 28
Shoots 12
Soil 4, 9, 14, 15, 17, 22, 27, 28
Spores 24, 25, 30
Stems 4, 12, 28, 30
Sunlight 6, 7, 8, 9, 16, 17

Temperature 17, 30
Trees 5, 8

Water 4, 6, 9, 10, 12, 13, 15, 17, 22, 24, 25, 28
Wilting 10, 30